VOCAL SELECTIONS FROM
Walt Disney's

# ALICE IN WONDERLAND

## Contents

| | |
|---|---|
| A-E-I-O-U (The Caterpillar Song) | 26 |
| Alice In Wonderland | 2 |
| All In The Golden Afternoon | 24 |
| The Caucus Race | 8 |
| How D'ye Do And Shake Hands | 12 |
| I'm Late | 6 |
| In A World Of My Own | 4 |
| March Of The Cards | 32 |
| 'Twas Brillig | 28 |
| The Unbirthday Song | 21 |
| Very Good Advice | 30 |
| The Walrus And The Carpenter | 14 |

ISBN 0-7935-0034-6

7777 W. BLUEMOUND RD. P.O. BOX 13819 MILWAUKEE, WI 53213

Art Copyright © 1984 Walt Disney Productions
Copyright © 1949, 1951 Walt Disney Music Company
Copyright Renewed
International Copyright Secured   All Rights Reserved

# Alice In Wonderland

Words by BOB HILLIARD

Music by SAMMY FAIN

**Slowly With Expression**

AL-ICE IN WON-DER-LAND, How do you get to won-der-land?

O-ver the hill or un-der-land or just be-hind the tree.

When clouds go roll-ing by, They roll a-way and leave the sky.

Copyright © 1951 by WALT DISNEY MUSIC COMPANY
International Copyright Renewed
All Rights Reserved   Used by Permission

# The Caucus Race

Words by
BOB HILLIARD

Music by
SAMMY FAIN

Ev - 'ry - bod - y take your place be - fore we start the caucus race.

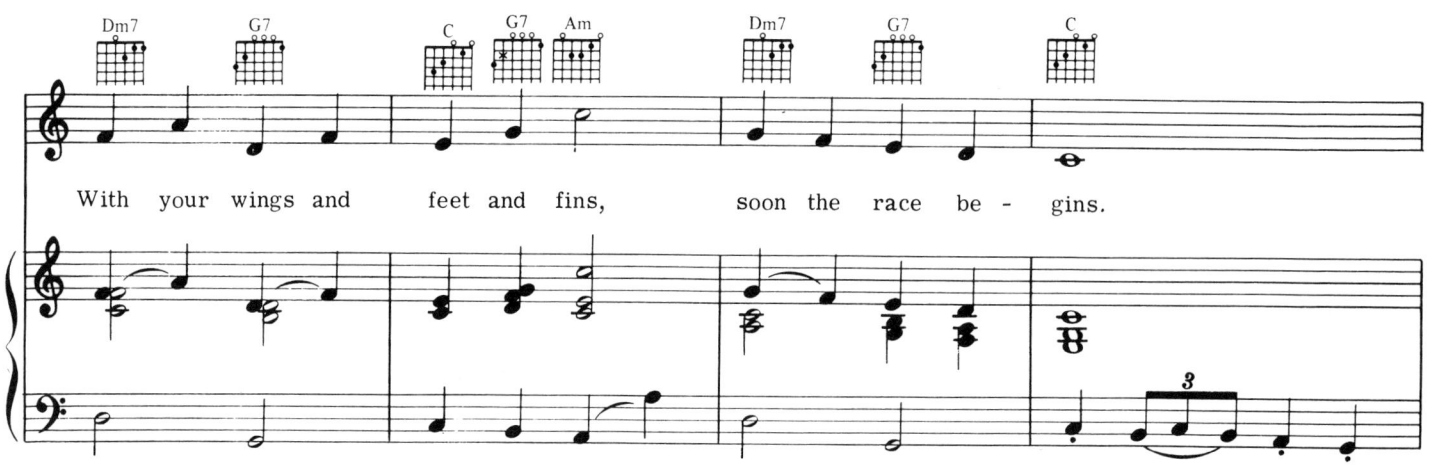

With your wings and feet and fins, soon the race be - gins.

Bugs and birds caught in the rain will race un - til they're dry a - gain. When you hear them

Copyright © 1949 by WALT DISNEY MUSIC COMPANY
International Copyright Renewed
All Rights Reserved   Used by Permission

# How D'ye Do And Shake Hands

By OLIVER WALLACE and CY COBEN

## Additional Verses

4. While at the wedding of some folks you hardly know by sight,
   And in a conversation with a woman on your right
   You say you think the bride's a mess, her face she ought to hide,
   And when you find you're talking to the mother of the bride, say: *(Refrain)*

5. While walking thru a cemetery very late at night
   You find that you're confronted by a figure dressed in white,
   And tho the blood inside your veins has quickly turned to ice
   Everything will be O.K. if you take my advice, say: *(Refrain)*

6. You walk into a restaurant as hungry as can be,
   And when you've had a meal of ev'rything from A to Z
   You realize you haven't got a single cent with you
   And when the manager comes over this is what you do, say: *(Refrain)*

7. You're speeding down the highway and the feeling is superb,
   And then you hear a siren and "Pull over to the curb",
   And when a cop who's big and tough comes walking up to you
   And asks you where the fire is that you are going to, say: *(Refrain)*

8. You go into a barbershop to get yourself a shave,
   And if you are the kind of guy who never can behave
   You ask the manicurist for a little kiss or two
   And then when you discover it's her husband shaving you, say: *(Refrain)*

*) *Always end with this Verse*
A handshake and a happy greeting's mighty hard to beat,
So at the risk of boring you I'm going to repeat
Remember in the future that no matter what you do
**Here's one way to get out of any mess you get into, say:** *(Refrain)*

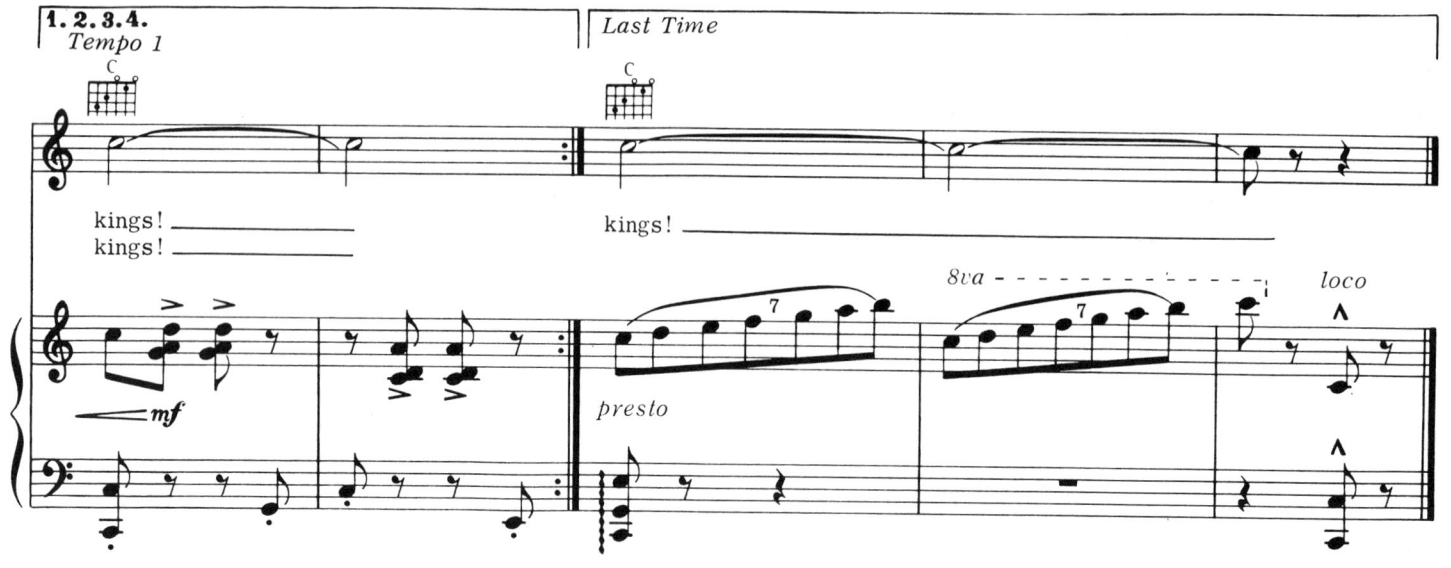

VERSE 3
    So the oysters went to follow and their shells and shoes were neat,
    But I fear my dear you'll find this queer, because they had no feet.
    Soon the oysters all were out of breath, and they said, let's stop and chat,
    'Cause most of us are ready to rest, you see, we're much too fat. (Fat..)

CHORUS
    The time has come, the Walrus said, to speak of other things,
    Of shoes and ships and sealing wax, of cabbages and kings,
    And why the sea is boiling hot, and whether pigs have wings,
    Callooh, callay, we eat today, like cabbages and kings.

VERSE 4
    Said the walrus, just a loaf of bread is exactly what we need,
    And some pepper and some vinegar and very good indeed.
    If you're ready little oyster friends, we can now begin the food,
    But not on us, the oysters all cried as they begun to plead. (Feed. . .)

CHORUS
    The time has come, the oysters cried, to speak of other things,
    Of shoes and ships and sealing wax, of cabbages and kings.
    And why the sea is boiling hot and whether pigs have wings.
    Callooh, callay, we're fools to play with cabbages and kings.

VERSE 5
    Oh, I weep for you, said the Walrus, and I deeply sympathize,
    Then he held his pocket handkerchief before his streaming eyes.
    Little oysters, said the Carpenter, but answer there came none,
    And this was scarcely odd because, they'd eaten every one.. (Oh . .)

CHORUS (Gradually faster and faster)
    The time has come, the Walrus said, to speak of other things,
    Of shoes and ships and sealing wax, of cabbages and kings.
    And why the sea is boiling hot and whether pigs have wings,
    Callooh, callay, a lucky day, for cabbages and kings.

On a lazy summer afternoon, young Alice becomes bored with her sister's reading of a history lesson. Feeling drowsy and dreamy, she sees a White Rabbit run by. Alice follows and tumbles headlong down his rabbit hole, landing in a mysterious underground room. There she finds a small door with a talking doorknob.

In A World Of My Own

The Doorknob tells her that by drinking from a bottle on the table she can quickly shrink in size and fit through the small door. Alice does so, but instead of shrinking, grows LARGER. Confused and annoyed, she weeps tears which fill the room. She drinks again from the bottle, and this time shrinks to a size so small that, riding within the bottle, she is swept on a wave of her own tears through the keyhole.

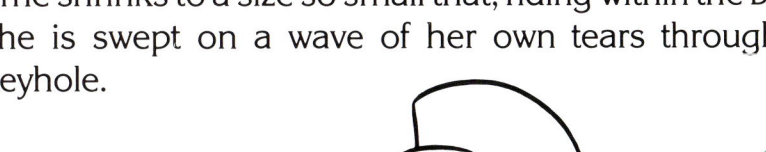

I'm Late

Alice is washed ashore to meet an odd group of characters playing a neverending game called a *Caucus Race*. Spotting the White Rabbit again, she sets out after him but is cornered by the very round Tweedledee and Tweedledum, who tell her a tale about the Walrus and the Carpenter.

The Tweedle twins then sing a farewell song as Alice continues chasing the White Rabbit. She soon finds his cozy home, and goes inside looking for him.

There, Alice eats a piece of candy, and grows so large that she splits the house apart, her arms and legs bursting through the doors and windows. The White Rabbit arrives and cries, "Monster...monster in my house!"

The Caucus Race

The Walrus And The Carpenter

How D'ye Do And Shake Hands

After an unsuccessful attempt by Bill the Lizard to free the "monster" from the house, Alice takes a nibble from a carrot growing in the Rabbit's garden and is again reduced in size.

A very small Alice now wanders into a garden of large, beautiful flowers...flowers that sing. They become suspicious of her, thinking she is some kind of weed, and drive her into the woods.

There, Alice encounters the Caterpillar smoking his hookah (a water pipe). He tells her she can grow taller by nibbling on a magic mushroom. Alice takes a bite and returns to her normal size.

Still on the trail of the White Rabbit, Alice enters a dark forest where she meets the Cheshire Cat, who is able to appear, disappear and create all sorts of different shapes and sizes at will. The Cheshire Cat directs Alice to the Mad Hatter's Tea Party where she hopes to find the White Rabbit.

At the Tea Party, Alice meets the Mad Hatter, March Hare and Dormouse and they celebrate a completely mad "un-birthday" party. Alice then leaves, having spotted the White Rabbit disappearing into the forest.

She follows him into the Tulgey Woods, where she meets the weirdest and strangest characters of all her adventures. She becomes lonely and frightened and begins to cry. The Cheshire Cat reappears and points the way to the palace of the Queen of Hearts.

A·E·I·O·U (The Caterpillar Song)

All In The Golden Afternoon

The Unbirthday Song

'Twas Brillig

Alice finds the Queen on the palace grounds and is invited to play croquet with Her Highness. The Cheshire Cat appears again to play pranks on the bad-tempered Queen, who orders executions all around. Alice is blamed for the pranks, but thanks to the King, is put on trial instead of being exectued.

The trial is peculiar and doesn't make sense to Alice, who escapes by running through a maze outside the royal court while being pursued by the Queen and her army of cards. Alice finds the rabbit hole and sees herself outside, sleeping under a tree. She frantically calls to herself to wake up just as the Queen and her army close in.

Alice awakens from her dream in "Wonderland," happy to be back in the real world where things make sense, even if they are a bit more unimaginative.

Very Good Advice

March Of The Cards

# A-E-I-O-U (The Caterpillar Song)

Music by OLIVER WALLACE

# 'Twas Brillig

From the poem by
Lewis Carroll

Words and Music by
DON RAYE
and GENE DE PAUL

Copyright © 1951 by WALT DISNEY MUSIC COMPANY
International Copyright Renewed
All Rights Reserved   Used by Permission

# March Of The Cards

By SAMMY FAIN